Read & Understand

ENGLISH COMPREHENSION

Shab

A BEGINNERS' SERIES

BOOK 5

priority PUBLICATIONS

priority
PUBLICATIONS

Published by Priority Publications
info@dspublishers.com
www.dspublishers.com

Eighth Impression 2018

9788180221224

Printed in India at
Beekam Print & Pack (P) Ltd.

Contents

ALL ABOUT OUR EARTH	5
WHALE	8
RUBBER	11
THE DONKEY AND THE DOG	14
THE RAILWAY	16
THE WOODPECKER	18
A COLD EVENING	20
MY BUS JOURNEY	23
PAUL AT SCHOOL	25
DICK AND MARY	27
AN OCTOPUS	30
HOW TO READ A MAP	32
THE FOOLISH DONKEY	34
THE FOUR SEASONS	36
THE ROBIN	38
A DAM	40
THE WISE GOATS	42

A RIVER	45
TENNIS	48
A DOG	50
THE TWO FROGS	52
CHICKADEE-DEE	54
THE NEIGHBOUR'S PARTY	56
VEGETABLES	58
THE BLUE BIRD	60
THE MEETING	62
MY MAGIC CARPET	64
REPTILES	66
THE JOLLY OLD CROW	68
THE HUNGRY MOUSE	70
A ROBOT	72
MY LOST DOLL	74
TRANSPORTATION	77

ALL ABOUT OUR EARTH

Our Earth is a sphere. It is round like a ball. Many years ago, people believed that Earth was flat. Later, it was found that if a person travelled all the way round the Earth, he would return to the same point from where he had started. This went on to prove that Earth was not flat but spherical.

The surface of Earth is made up of land and water. The areas of land are called continents and the large bodies of water are called oceans. The point that is farthest north is known as the North Pole and the point that is farthest south is called the South Pole.

The Earth rotates on its axis, from west to east. We do not feel the movement because everything on the Earth spins with it. Our Earth takes twenty-four hours to complete one rotation. It revolves around the Sun in a path called the Orbit. It takes 365 days to complete one revolution. Earth is a wonderful place. It is the home for many living things.

Fill in the blanks:

1) Our Earth is a ______________.

2) Many years ago, people ______________ that Earth was flat.

3) If a person __________ all the way round the Earth, he would return to the same _______ from where he had _____________.

4) The surface of Earth is made up of ________ and __________.

5) The point that is __________ north is known as the ___________ Pole.

Strike out (✗) the incorrect option:

1) The surface of Earth is made up of......

(a) land and water (b) air and fire

2) The areas of land are called......

(a) oceans (b) continents

3) The large bodies of water are called......

(a) oceans (b) mountains

4) The point that is farthest south is called......

(a) the South Pole (b) Axis

5) The Earth rotates on its axis, from......

(a) east to west (b) west to east

6) It revolves around the ...... in an Orbit.

(a) Sun (b) Axis

WHALE

A whale is a huge sea animal, which looks like a fish. But whales are not fish. They belong to a group of animals called marine mammals. The blue whale is the largest animal that has ever lived on Earth.

In early days, people killed whales for their meat and for oil. The whale oil was used for lamps and also for cooking. Today, different parts of the whale are used to make fertilizer, glue, soap, and medicines.

Whales have a thick body and a very huge head. Their skin is smooth and rubbery, so that they can slip easily through water. Beneath the skin there is a layer of fat called blubber. This fat keeps them warm in cold water. Whale oil is obtained from these blubbers.

Whales can stay under the water for long periods without breathing. They come up to the surface of the water to breathe. It is a beautiful sight to see a whale leap out of the water to get a breath of air.

Whales live in large groups, called pods. They communicate with one another by making some sounds. Whales have teeth. They eat fish, squid and seals. Some whales eat water plants.

Circle the correct spelling:

1) (a) Whales (b) Whails (c) Whaels

2) (a) Marien (b) Marine (c) Mareen

3) (a) Killd (b) Kiled (c) Killed

4) (a) Smooth (b) Smouth (c) Smuoth

5) (a) Eesily (b) Eisily (c) Easily

6) (a) Blubber (b) Bluber (c) Blubbar

Answer in one line:

1) Which group of animals do the whales belong to?

Ans ____________________

2) In early days, why did people kill the whales?

Ans ____________________

3) What type of skin do the whales have?

Ans ____________________

4) What is the blubber?

Ans ____________________

5) What keeps the whales warm in cold water?

Ans ____________________

6) What is a group of whales called?

Ans ____________________

RUBBER

Rubber is an elastic substance made from the juice of a tree. It holds air and keeps out moisture. It is air-tight and water-tight.

Rubber is useful in making tyres and tubes, which are used on cars, buses, trucks, bicycles and aeroplanes. It is also used for making boots, raincoats, gloves, hot water bags, ice bags, syringe, surgeons' gloves, elastic tapes, toys, elastic bands, cushions, pillows and mattresses. Oxygen tent also has parts made of rubber. Swimmers wear

bathing suits and caps made of rubber. They even sunbathe on rubber rafts. Many sports are played with rubber balls.

Rubber comes from rubber trees. Workers called 'tappers' collect a white juice called 'latex' from the rubber tree. The tappers cut a narrow slanting groove in the bark of the tree and keep a cup below it. The latex flows down into the cup drop by drop. It is then poured into large pots and taken to the factory where it is made into dry rubber. Rubber plantations are found in Malaysia, Indonesia, India, Sri Lanka, Burma and China.

Make sentences of your own:

1) Rubber: ______________________________

2) Juice : ______________________________

3) Tree : ______________________________

4) Groove : ______________________________

Write True (T) or False (F):

1) Rubber is an elastic substance obtained from fish. ( )

2) It is used for making raincoats, gloves, boots and ice bags. ( )

3) Oxygen tent also has parts made of rubber. ( )

4) The white juice obtained from the rubber tree is called 'tappers'. ( )

5) The workers cut a narrow slanting groove in the bark of the tree. ( )

6) Rubber keeps out moisture. ( )

7) The latex flows down into the cup drop by drop. ( )

8) It is useful in making tyres and tubes. ( )

THE DONKEY AND THE DOG

A man had a little dog. He would give the dog biscuits and milk, and would lovingly pat his head. The dog also loved his master. He would follow him everywhere, wagging his tail. Sometimes, the dog would sit on his master's lap.

The man also had a donkey, who was envious of the dog. "My master never pats on my head or plays with me," he would think. "The dog doesn't do any work, still he gets all the love of the master."

One day, the donkey decided to play with the master the same way as he had seen the dog do. He ran into his master's room,

braying loudly. Suddenly, he knocked over a flower vase and broke it. The master, who had been sleeping, woke up terrified and cried for help. The neighbours came with sticks and beat up the donkey, thinking he had gone mad. The foolish donkey had to run away from there to save his life.

Complete the sentences:

1) The man would give ____________________________ ____________ milk.

2) The dog would follow him _____________________ _________________ tail.

3) Sometimes, the dog would ___________________ ______________ lap.

4) The man also had ______________________________ ______________ dog.

5) One day, the donkey ____________________________ _______ master.

6) He ran into his __________________________________ ______________ loudly.

THE RAILWAY

The railway is one of the most important means of transport. Every day, thousands of trains run along the railway tracks throughout the world, carrying passengers and goods. A train carrying people is called 'Passenger Train' and the one carrying goods is called 'Goods Train'.

The passengers travel to small towns as well as to large cities. Many of them travel on the local trains daily to their workplace and back home.

Unlike aeroplanes, cars and ships, trains are not steered. They use two strong steel rails to guide them along a permanent route. The guard instructs the driver to start the train. Signals are used to control the train and to prevent accidents. Red colour means 'stop', yellow means 'get ready' and green means 'proceed'. Powerful diesel or electric locomotives move the trains along the track. There are many coaches to accomodate the travellers.

Fill in the blanks:

1) Trains carry passengers to small __________ and large _________.

2) The __________ instructs the driver to _____________ the train.

3) Signals are used to_____________the train.

4) The railway is one of the most important means of __________.

5) A train carrying people is called __________________ .

6) Some passengers travel daily to their ________________and back home.

THE WOODPECKER

I'm a woodpecker, a bird
Whose sound through wood and dale is heard;
I tap, tap, tap, with noisy glee,
To test the bark of every tree.

I saw a rainbow stretching gay,
Across the sky, the other day;
And someone said, "Goodbye to rain,
The woodpecker has come again."

Match the following:

1) I'm a woodpecker	(a) with noisy glee
2) Whose sound through wood	(b) come again
3) I tap, tap, tap	(c) a bird
4) Across the sky	(d) and dale is heard
5) And someone said	(e) the other day
6) To test the bark	(f) stretching gay
7) I saw a rainbow	(g) of every tree
8) The woodpecker has	(h) Goodbye to rain

A COLD EVENING

It was a cold, winter day. I had a special class and so I had to be in the school till five o'clock. When I came out, it was drizzling and I felt very cold. The school bus had already left without me. I knew the way home, so I started walking slowly.

I was shivering with cold and I didn't have an umbrella with me. The roads were deserted as everyone preferred staying indoors. I took forty-five minutes to reach home.

My mother was very worried because I hadn't reached home at the usual time. She felt relieved only when she saw me. She changed my wet clothes and asked me to wear some warm clothes.

My mother gave me a hot cup of tea. Then she made me lie down on the bed and covered me with warm blankets. I felt very cozy and happy, with my mother sitting close to me, holding me with both her hands.

Rewrite the paragraph, using the appropriate punctuation marks:

it was a cold winter day i had a special class and so i had to be in the school till five o clock when i came out it was drizzling and i felt very cold the school bus had already left without me i knew the way home so i started walking slowly i was shivering with cold and I didnt have an umbrella with me

Fill in the blanks:

1) I had a ______________ class.

2) When I came out, it was ______________.

3) The school bus had ____________ left without me.

4) I was ___________ with cold and I didn't have an ____________ with me.

5) The roads were _______________ as everyone ____________ staying indoors.

6) My mother was very ____________ because I hadn't ____________ home at the usual time.

7) She felt ____________ only when she saw me.

8) She gave me a hot cup of ________.

9) She covered me with warm ______________.

10) I felt very cozy and ___________.

MY BUS JOURNEY

I was very happy when my father told me he would take me to his friend's house by bus. I had never travelled by a bus before. We waited at the bus stop. When the bus arrived, I was in a hurry to get in. My father told me that I should never try to get into a moving bus. We got a side seat. My father told me not to put my head or hands outside the window. "You have to be careful while getting off the bus. Let it stop first," he said. "Always try to offer your seat if you see an elderly man or woman standing."

My father also told me that I must buy the ticket. "People travelling without tickets are punished," he said. I hope one day I will get a chance to travel on a bus by myself. I will always remember what my father has told me while traveling.

Strike out (✗) the incorrect option:

1) My father took me to his ...... house.

(a) friend's (b) brother's

2) I had never travelled by a ...... before.

(a) car (b) bus

3) When the bus ...... I was in a hurry to get in.

(a) arrived (b) left

4) My father told me that I must buy the......

(a) ticket (b) banana

5) People travelling without tickets are......

(a) rewarded (b) punished

PAUL AT SCHOOL

Paul is a good boy. He is very punctual; he never misses his school bus. He is always neat and tidy; he wears clean uniform and polished shoes. His books are well covered and neat; he never scribbles on them.

Paul tries to keep his classroom tidy. He picks up the bits of paper strewn around and throws them into the waste paper bin. He never borrows pens or pencils from others, and never fights with his friends. His teachers also like him because he is good in studies and does his homework regularly. No wonder Paul gets the good conduct certificate every year!

Match the following:

1) Paul is a	(a) with his friends
2) His books are	(b) into the waste paper bin
3) He throws the bits of paper	(c) in studies
4) He never scribbles	(d) regularly
5) He is good	(e) his school bus
6) He does his homework	(f) on his books
7) He never misses	(g) well covered and neat
8) He never fights	(h) good boy

DICK AND MARY

Dick and Mary were very naughty children. One day, when their parents had gone out, they decided to go and see the world outside.

Dick asked Mary, "Shall we go to the seaside? We can play in the waves and collect some seashells also." Mary was very happy. So, both set off for the seaside. They walked and walked but there was no seaside to be seen. It was getting late. Mary said, "I am tired; I can't walk any longer." Even Dick was tired. They did not know how to get home. They sat on the pavement and began to cry.

A lady passing by saw them and asked, "Why are you crying, children?" Dick replied, "We have lost our way. We don't know how to get back home." While they were talking, they saw their parents walking towards them. They had come searching for their children because they did not find them at home. Dick and Mary were very happy to see their parents. They said, "We will be good children, and we will never go out alone."

Make sentences of your own:

1) Play : ______________________________

2) Waves : ______________________________

3) Walk : ______________________________

4) Tired : ______________________________

5) Home : ______________________________

6) Good : ______________________________

Tick (✓) the correct answer:

1) What kind of children were Dick and Mary?

(a) They were very naughty. ☐

(b) They were very quiet. ☐

2) What did they decide one day?

(a) They decided to go outside. ☐

(b) They decided to sleep. ☐

3) Where did they set off for?

(a) They set off for the seaside. ☐

(b) They set off for the lakeside. ☐

4) Why did they sit on the pavement?

(a) They had lost their way. ☐

(b) They did not want to go home. ☐

5) What did they see?

(a) They saw an elephant. ☐

(b) They saw their parents walking towards them. ☐

AN OCTOPUS

An octopus is a sea animal, found on the muddy bottom of the ocean and also in rocky and sandy places in shallow water. Its body is round and boneless, and it has eight long arms called 'tentacles'. It uses these arms to move along the waters and also to capture small insects. If it loses one arm, a new arm grows in its place.

The octopus has two large eyes on each side of the head. Its mouth looks like a beak. It eats crabs and snails. To escape from the enemy, it swims backwards and throws out some fluid to scare the enemy. Sometimes, it escapes from the enemy by changing its colour. In some countries, octopuses are eaten as food.

Fill in the blanks:

1) An octopus is a sea __________, found on the muddy __________ of the ocean.

2) Its body is round and __________.

3) It has eight long arms called __________.

4) It uses these __________ to move along the waters and also to __________ small insects.

5) The octopus has two __________ eyes on each side of the __________.

6) To escape from the enemy, it swims __________ and throws out some __________.

HOW TO READ A MAP

My school is at Mount Street. It is a wide road. When you enter the road, you can see the big school gate. From the gate, you can see the main building. You can go straight and enter the hall. You can see a long corridor on the left side. You can turn to right for the office room. The library is opposite the office room. There are three classrooms next to the office room. My classroom is the one in the centre. All the other classrooms are on the first floor and second floor. We have a big playground in front of the main building.

Write 'RIGHT' or 'WRONG' in the boxes:

1) My school is at Mount Street, which is a narrow lane. [ ]

2) When you enter the road, you can see the big school gate. [ ]

3) From the gate, you cannot see the main building. [ ]

4) There is a long corridor on the right side. [ ]

5) If you go straight, you can enter the hall. [ ]

6) The library is opposite the office room. [ ]

7) All the other classrooms are on the first floor and second floor. [ ]

8) There are three classrooms next to the office room. [ ]

THE FOOLISH DONKEY

Once, there lived a salt merchant and his donkey. Everyday, the merchant would load sacks of salt on the donkey and lead him to the town, to sell the salt. On the way, they would cross a stream. One day, as they were crossing the stream, the donkey slipped and fell into the water. When he got up, he found his load lighter because the salt had melted in the water. He got an idea. Next time when they were on their way to the town again, the donkey deliberately fell into the water. From that day, he made it a habit.

Now the merchant had a doubt. He decided to teach the donkey a lesson. On their next trip, the merchant loaded the donkey with sacks of cotton. When they reached the stream, the donkey as usual fell into the water. But this time, the load became heavier, since the cotton had soaked water. The donkey had a tough time carrying the load to the town. From that day, he never tried to cheat the merchant; he had learned a good lesson.

Complete the paragraphs:

Once, there lived a salt ____________ and his donkey. ______________, the merchant would load _________ of salt on the __________ and lead him to the _________, to sell the salt. On the way, they would _________ a stream.

One day, as they were crossing the ______, the donkey slipped and fell into the ________. When he got up, he _________ his load lighter because the _______ had ________ in the water. He got an _____. Next time when they were on their _______ to the town ________, the donkey ________________ fell into the water.

THE FOUR SEASONS

There are four seasons in a year – Summer, Winter, Rainy and Spring. Summer season is very hot. We sit under the fan and drink plenty of water. We carry umbrella while going out. Some rivers and ponds get dried up.

Winter season is cold. We wear woollen clothes and use warm blankets when we go to sleep. Nights during winter are colder than day.

We get clouds, rain, thunder and lightning during the rainy season. The rivers and ponds get filled up with water. We carry umbrellas and raincoats when we go out.

Spring season brings flowers. We see blooming flowers and fresh green leaves on the trees. Birds sing and the butterflies flutter their wings, making the weather pleasant.

Make appropriate pairs:

1) Summer season	(a) Rain
2) Rainy season	(b) Flowers
3) Winter season	(c) Hot
4) Spring season	(d) Cold

Circle the correct spelling:

1)	(a) Summar	(b) Sammer	(c) Summer
2)	(a) Winter	(b) Wintar	(c) Wintur
3)	(a) Thunder	(b) Thander	(c) Thundar
4)	(a) Raincot	(b) Reincot	(c) Raincoat

THE ROBIN

I am a robin, very brown
And big and plump
And smooth and round.

My breast is pretty, bright and red;
And see this top-knot on my head!

I heard the boys awhile ago
Shooting robins o'er the snow;

And flew away
in trembling fear.
And thought I'd hide
from them in here.

Match the following:

1) I am a robin	(a) in trembling fear
2) And big and plump	(b) And smooth and round
3) My breast is pretty	(c) awhile ago
4) And see this top-knot	(d) from them in here
5) I heard the boys	(e) on my head
6) Shooting robins	(f) very brown
7) And flew away	(g) o'er the snow
8) And thought I'd hide	(h) bright and red

A DAM

A dam is a barrier built to contain water and also to stop the flow of water. The high barrier which is placed across the river prevents flooding also. It stores the water, forming a lake or a reservoir.

The stored water can be used in many ways. When rivers or streams become dry, the stored water can be used for irrigation. The water which falls from a great height produces electric power, which is used in homes and industries. Water can be released through outlets when the valves are opened. Dams are useful in countries where there is low or irregular rainfall.

Fill in the blanks:

1) The ________ water is used in many ways.

2) When rivers or ___________ become dry, the stored water can be used for ______________.

3) The water which falls from a great _________ produces ____________ power.

4) Water can be ______________ through outlets when the ______________ are opened.

Rewrite the paragraph, using the appropriate punctuation marks:

a dam is a barrier built to contain water and also to stop the flow of water the high barrier which is placed across the river prevents flooding also it stores the water forming a lake or a reservoir

____

____

____

____

____

THE WISE GOATS

One day, a goat was walking along the woods. She came upon a river and had to cross a narrow wooden bridge to reach the other side.

When the goat was halfway on the bridge, she saw another goat coming from the opposite side. The bridge was so narrow that only one goat could pass at a time. So, the first goat said to the second goat, "You go back, so that I can cross the bridge." "Why don't you go back?" said the second goat.

Both of them started to fight as neither of them wanted to go back. Soon, they realised that there was no end to their argument. "If we go on fighting like this, we both will fall into the stream and die," they said.

So, the wise goats thought of a plan. One of them lay flat on the plank of the bridge while the other stepped on her and crossed over the bridge. The other goat also went her way. In this way, they solved their problem in a friendly way.

Make sentences of your own:

1) Woods : ______________________________

2) River : ______________________________

3) Bridge : ______________________________

4) Fight : ______________________________

5) Wise : ______________________________

Tick (✓) the correct answer:

1) What did the first goat see when she was halfway on the bridge?

(a) She saw a dog. ☐

(b) She saw another goat. ☐

2) What kind of bridge it was?

(a) It was an iron bridge. ☐

(b) It was a wooden bridge. ☐

3) Was the bridge very wide?

(a) No, it was very narrow. ☐

(b) Yes. ☐

4) What did the first goat ask the second goat to do?

(a) She asked her to jump down. ☐

(b) She asked her to go back. ☐

5) What happened in the end?

(a) Both of them drowned. ☐

(b) They solved their problem in a friendly way. ☐

A RIVER

A river is a large body of water that flows over the land. A river begins its journey from high mountains or hills. As it flows, it gets more water from streams, lakes, springs, other rivers and rainfall. The end of the river where the water flows into an ocean or lake is called its mouth.

Some rivers are very small; they dry up during hot season. Rivers are useful for trade, transportation and irrigation. The force of the flowing water at waterfalls is used to generate electricity. Some of the longest rivers in the world are the Nile river in Africa and the Amazon river in South America.

Strike out (✗) the incorrect option:

1) A river is a large body of......

(a) water (b) land

2) It begins its journey from......

(a) ocean (b) mountains

3) Some rivers dry up during......

(a) rainy season (b) hot season

4) The flowing water is used to generate......

(a) electricity (b) machinery

5) A river gets more water from......

(a) wells (b) streams

6) The end of the river is called its......

(a) belly (b) mouth

Underline the Articles and Verbs:

A river is a large body of water that flows over the land. A river begins its journey from high mountains or hills. As it flows, it gets more water from streams, lakes, springs, other rivers and rainfall. The end of the river where the water flows into an ocean or lake is called its mouth. Some rivers are very small; they dry up during hot season.

Make at least two meaningful words using the jumbled letters:

1) ainsmoutn ______________ ______________

2) rafallin ______________ ______________

3) ngsspri ______________ ______________

4) watallerf ______________ ______________

5) rategene ______________ ______________

TENNIS

Tennis is an outdoor game. It is played with a racket and a ball. The ball is hollow, but the racket is very heavy. The game between two players is called "Singles" and the one between four players is called "Doubles". The tennis court is divided into two equal sides by a net in the middle. The players stand on each side. When a player is not able to return the ball properly, the other person scores points.

The players attend various tournaments held every year. The Wimbledon championship is one of the world's major tournaments. People watch the matches with excitement. Some people play tennis to stay fit and healthy.

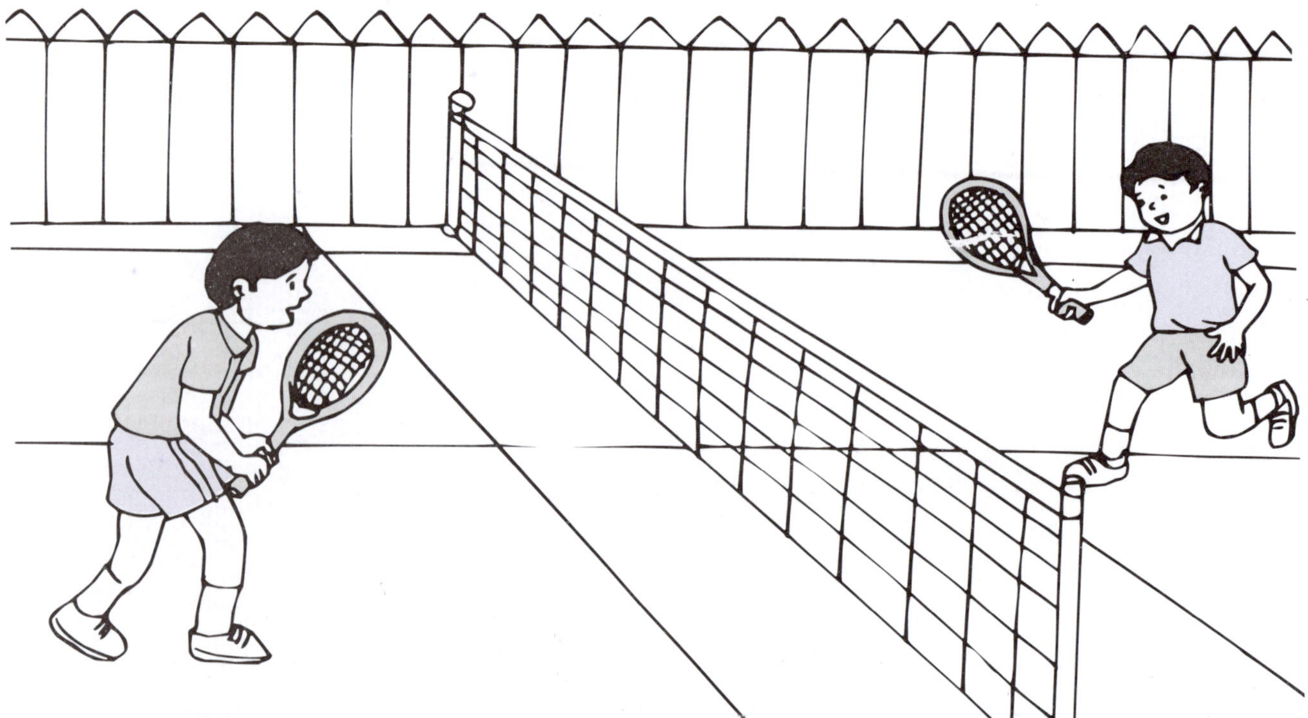

Fill in the blanks:

1) Tennis is an ____________________ game.

2) It is played with a __________ and a _______.

3) The ball is __________, but the racket is very ___________.

4) The game between _______ players is called "Singles".

5) The game between four players is called _____________.

6) The tennis court is _________ into two equal sides by a _________ in the middle.

7) The players attend various _______________ held every year.

8) People watch the matches with __________.

A DOG

Dogs are a popular pet throughout the world. They are intelligent and loyal. Many people keep dogs for company.

Some dogs are trained to help people; they guide the blind and deaf. Such dogs are called "guide dogs". A blind person can take his dog to shops, restaurants and hotels. The guide dog learns to watch traffic and helps the person to cross the road safely.

A dog's sense of smell helps it to recognize objects. It can also hear sounds at much greater distance. Dogs perform in circuses, on stage, in movies and on the television. People watch the obedience test of dogs at dog shows.

Doberman and mastiffs are used as police dogs. St. Bernard is famous for rescuing people from danger. Terriers are kept as watch dogs. A dog is a man's friend.

Write 'RIGHT' or 'WRONG' in the boxes:

1) Dogs are a popular pet throughout the world. ☐

2) None of the dogs are intelligent or loyal. ☐

3) Some dogs are trained to guide the blind and deaf. ☐

4) The guide dogs do not learn to watch traffic. ☐

5) A dog's sense of smell helps it to recognize objects. ☐

6) Doberman and mastiffs are used as police dogs. ☐

THE TWO FROGS

Two frogs lived in a small village. They had heard a lot about the city. So, one day they set off to see the city. It was a very hot day. After hopping a few miles, they felt tired. One of them asked the other, "Can you see the city?" The other replied, "No, but I think I might be able to see it if I climb on you." So, he climbed on the other's back and turned around. His eyes could see only what was behind... and that was their village! "Do you see the city?" asked the frog from below. "Yes, but it looks just like our village," replied the frog on top. So, they decided to return to their village. Later, they told the other frogs, "We saw the city. It is just like our village."

Answer in one line:

1) Why did the frogs set off to the city?

Ans ______________________________

2) Why did they feel tired?

Ans ______________________________

3) What did one of them ask the other?

Ans ______________________________

4) What did the frog on top see?

Ans ______________________________

5) Why did the frogs return to their village?

Ans ______________________________

6) What did they tell the other frogs?

Ans ______________________________

CHICKADEE-DEE

Little darling of the snow,
Careless how the winds may blow,
Happy as a bird can be,
Singing, oh, so cheerily,
Chickadee-dee! Chickadee-dee!

When the skies are cold and gray,
When he trills his happiest lay,
Through the clouds he seems to see,
Hidden things to you and me,
Chickadee-dee! Chickadee-dee!

Very likely little birds
Have their thoughts too deep for word,
But we know, and all agree,
That the world would dreary be
Without birds, dear Chickadee!

Word Meanings:

1) Chickadee - A small bird
2) Trill - Sound of a bird singing
3) Lay - Song
4) Dreary - Gloomy

Complete the lines:

1) Little darling ______________________________.

2) Careless ______________________________.

3) Happy as a ______________________________.

4) When the skies ______________________________.

5) When he trills ______________________________.

6) Through the ______________________________.

7) Have their thoughts ______________________________.

8) But we know ______________________________.

THE NEIGHBOUR'S PARTY

Our neighbour held a party last night. The guests parked their cars in front of the other houses, blocking their gates. They played loud music. The neighbouring children could not study; small babies, sick and elderly people could not sleep because of the blaring music.

The guests had a good time and then dumped all the leftovers of the dinner on the roadside. The area was full of garbage.

The next day, we went to their house and told them, "We are your neighbours. We always try to keep our street clean. We never throw the rubbish on the

road. We throw them into the garbage bin. We are your friends. Please try to keep the place clean." the rubbish on the road. We throw them into the garbage bin. We are your friends. Please try to keep the place clean." The neighbour replied, "We are terribly sorry. We will never do such a thing again. We will always keep the place clean."

Fill in the blanks:

1) Our ______________ held a party last night.

2) The guests _______ their cars in front of the other houses, ____________ their gates.

3) The _____________ children could not study.

4) Small _________, sick and elderly __________ could not sleep ___________ of the music.

5) The guests dumped all the __________ of the dinner on the _____________.

6) The area was full of ___________________.

VEGETABLES

Vegetables are an important part of a healthy diet. We use them –raw or cooked– as part of a main meal or in salads, soups and snacks. They contain iron, vitamins, minerals and calcium. Many vegetables can be grown in a kitchen garden.

Different parts of a plant, such as bulbs, flowers, leaves, roots, stems, seeds, and tubers, are used as vegetables. Onion is a bulb, it grows under the ground; cauliflower is a flower; tomato is a fruit; beetroot and carrot are roots; peas and corn are seeds; and potato is a tuber. Vegetable oil is obtained from certain vegetables. Sunflower oil, soya oil and coconut oil are used for cooking.

Match the following:

1) We use them	(a) tuber
2) Vegetables are an important part	(b) are used for cooking
3) Different parts of a plant are	(c) under the ground
4) Beetroot and carrot are	(d) seeds
5) Onion is a	(e) raw or cooked
6) Peas and corn are	(f) used as vegetables
7) Potato is a	(g) in a kitchen garden
8) Onion grows	(h) of a healthy diet
9) Many vegetables can be grown	(i) bulb
10) Soya oil and sunflower oil	(j) roots

THE BLUE BIRD

I'm a blue bird don't you see
Me sitting on this apple tree.

I left my nest an hour ago
To look for bugs and worms, you know.

And now I know the very thing
That while I'm waiting I will sing...
Oh! beautiful and balmy spring.

Rewrite the poem arranging the lines in the correct order:

1) That while I'm waiting I will sing...
To look for bugs and worms, you know.

2) And now I know the very thing
Me sitting on this apple tree.

3) I'm a blue bird don't you see
I left my nest an hour ago
Oh! beautiful and balmy spring.

1) ______________________________
____

2) ______________________________
____

3) ______________________________
____
____

THE MEETING

There was a big meeting on the playground. The members were balls of different sports. They had assembled there for a talk.

They were free because it was raining and so no one had gone to play. The football spoke, "Thank God, no one is kicking me today. The players kick me all over again and again. I just survive because I have a tough body." "What about me?" said the tennis ball. "They beat me with a strong bat."

The golf ball spoke gently, "I don't have many problems. I always take a few seconds' rest when I go into the hole." The cricket ball, who kept quiet all this time, spoke, "Well, I am not spared even in heavy rains. They mop all the water and cover the ground. Later, they continue the game. But isn't it fun to hear the people cheering at us!" Hearing this, all the other balls started smiling. "Yes, yes!" they said in unison. "Its real fun!" And the meeting ended on a happy note.

Fill in the blanks:

1) There was a big meeting on the ____________.

2) The balls were free because it was ________ and so no one had gone to ________.

3) The ___________ spoke, "Thank God, no one is kicking me _________.

4) I just ________ because I have a tough body.

5) The golf ball spoke ________, "I don't have many problems.

6) The ___________ ball, who kept quiet all this time, spoke, "Well, I am not _________ even in ________ rains.

MY MAGIC CARPET

I have a magic carpet
It's made of satin soft;
I can sit or sleep alike
When it flies to places I like.
It takes me through the gardens,
I can smell the wild blossoms,
When it flies me through the woods,
I pluck the berries and fruits.
It takes me up the mountains
It flies me through the clouds;
And I can view the rainbow,
With all its beautiful colours.
I've seen the mighty ocean
The foamy waves and rocks;
The ships sailing on the waters
And the children playing on the sands.

Match the following:

1) I have a magic carpet	a) And the children playing on the sands.
2) I can sit or sleep alike	b) It flies me through the clouds;
3) It takes me	c) through the woods,
4) When it flies me	d) through the gardens,
5) It takes me up the mountains	e) When it flies to places I like.
6) And I can view the rainbow,	f) The foamy waves and rocks;
7) I've seen the mighty ocean	g) With all its beautiful colours.
8) The ships sailing on the waters	h) It's made of satin soft;

REPTILES

A reptile is an animal with dry and scaly skin. Lizards, crocodiles, snakes and turtles are reptiles. They breathe through the lungs. Many reptiles become active and move about at night. Some reptiles live a long life. Turtles live up to hundred years.

Some large lizards live in deserts. Many snakes and crocodiles live in water. Most reptiles eat other animals. Some lizards and turtles eat only plants. Snakes can go without food for long periods. Some lizards escape from their enemy by changing their colours. They can change their colour to match the surroundings. Some snakes lie motionless, pretending to be dead, to deceive the enemy.

Answer in one line:

1) What type of skin does a reptile have?

Ans ____________________________________

2) How do lizards escape from their enemy?

Ans ____________________________________

3) When do the reptiles move about?

Ans ____________________________________

Fill in the blanks:

1) A reptile breathes through the __________.

2) Crocodiles live in ________________.

3) Turtles live up to ________________ years.

4) Some large lizards live in ______________.

5) Some _________ and turtles eat only plants.

6) Most reptiles eat other ________________.

THE JOLLY OLD CROW

On the limb of a tree, sat a Jolly old crow,
And chattered away with glee, with glee;
As he saw the old farmer go out to sow,
And he cried: "It's all for me, for me...
Caw, caw, caw!
I've learned all the tricks
of this wonderful man,
Who has such a regard for the crow,
the crow;
That he lays out his grounds
in a regular plan,
And covers his corn in a row, a row...
Caw, caw, caw!"

Word Meanings:

1) Limb - Branch of a tree
2) Chatter - Talk fast
3) Glee - Joy
4) Sow - Scatter the seeds

Rearrange the jumbled words and write the lines in the correct order:

1) learned I've all tricks the
wonderful of man this ,
has such Who a regard the for crow,
crow the;

2) he That lays his out grounds
regular in a plan,
And his corn covers in row, a a row...
Caw, caw, caw!

1) ______________________________
____
____
____

2) ______________________________
____
____
____

THE HUNGRY MOUSE

A mouse had not eaten any food for many days. He became very thin and weak. One day, he saw an urn full of corn. "Ah, my favourite food," thought the mouse. He found a small hole in the urn and crept into it. The hungry mouse went on and on eating the juicy corn. So delighted he was that he could not stop, until he finished all the corn.

But, now he became so fat that he could not come out of the urn. Seeing him struggle in the hole, another mouse said, "Better be inside, friend! If you don't eat for a few days, you will become thin again. Then you can easily crawl out of the hole."

Answer in one line:

1) Why did the mouse become thin?

Ans ______________________________

2) What did he see one day?

Ans ______________________________

3) Why couldn't he come out of the urn?

Ans ______________________________

Complete the paragraph:

A mouse had not eaten any ________ for many days. He ___________ very thin and weak. One day, he saw an _______ full of _________. He found a small ____________ in the urn and __________ into it. The ____________ mouse went on and on eating the _______________ corn. So delighted he was that he could not __________, until he ______________ all the corn.

A ROBOT

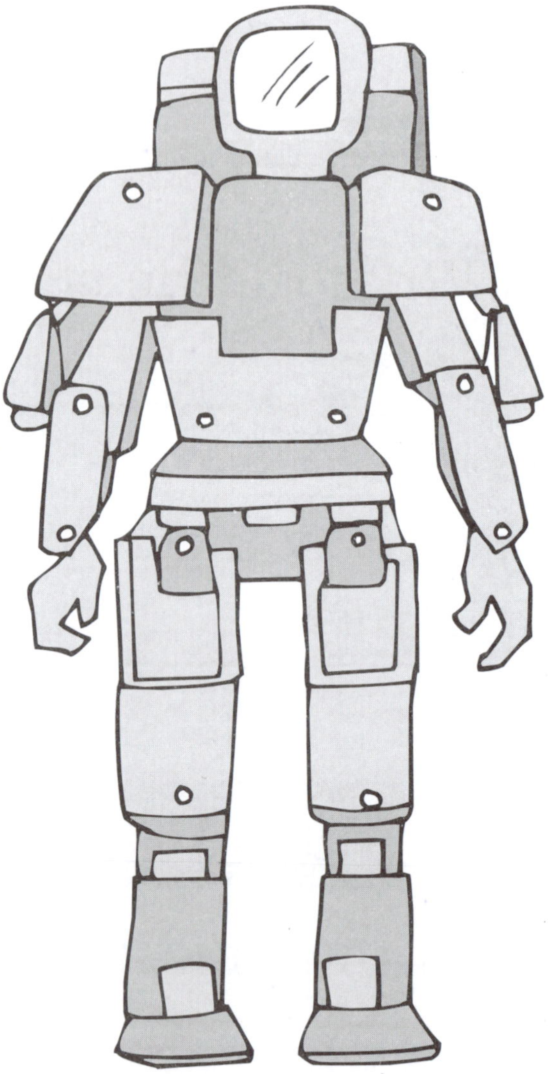

A robot is a mechanical device that operates automatically. It performs many jobs. Sometimes, we find some jobs boring, difficult or dangerous. Such jobs are assigned to the robots.

Certain robots are designed to do welding, drilling and painting. Some can even assemble small electronic gadgets. A robot functions by following a set of instructions. These instructions are stored in the computer of the robot. Most robots use a single arm to lift objects and use tools.

Some robots are equipped with television cameras. Scientists feel that such robots can be used for carrying out the complicated and dangerous jobs like the sea-floor research.

Write 'RIGHT' or 'WRONG' in the boxes:

1) A robot is a mechanical device that operates automatically. [ ]

2) None of the robots are designed to do welding or drilling. [ ]

3) Some robots can assemble small electronic gadgets. [ ]

4) Jobs that are boring or difficult are assigned to the robots. [ ]

5) Most robots use a single arm to lift objects and use tools. [ ]

6) Some robots are equipped with television cameras. [ ]

7) Robots cannot be used for carrying out the complicated and dangerous research jobs. [ ]

8) Robots do not follow any set of instructions. [ ]

MY LOST DOLL

My mother had given me a beautiful doll for my birthday last year. I used to carry my doll wherever I went. I called her 'Jennie'.

Last Friday when I came back from school, my doll was missing. I searched everywhere but could not find her. I thought she had left me, and so I began to cry. My father said he would buy me another doll, but I wanted only my Jennie. She was the most favourite of all my toys.

Today was my birthday. I got many presents from my friends and relatives. I saw a big packet wrapped in silver paper, decorated with blue ribbon. I slowly opened it. I was so surprised to see my dear Jennie lying in the packet.

Later, my mother told me that she had got Jennie from under my bed. She wanted to give me a surprise, so she did not tell me about it. I hugged my mother and thanked her. The day I got my Jennie back was the happiest day of my life.

Make at least two meaningful words using the jumbled letters:

1) bthirdya ____________ ____________

2) isendfr ____________ ____________

3) realsitev ____________ ____________

4) corateded ____________ ____________

Fill in the blanks:

1) My doll's name was _______________.

2) Last ________ when I came back from school, my doll was ____________.

3) I ___________ everywhere but could not find Jenny.

4) My ___________ said he would ___________ me another doll.

5) Jennie was the most _____________ of all my toys.

6) I got many _____________ from my friends.

7) I saw a big packet __________ in silver paper.

8) It was decorated with _____________ ribbon.

TRANSPORTATION

Transportation means the moving of people and goods from one place to another. Without transportation there will not be any trade and without trade there will not be any towns or cities.

In earlier days, people walked long distances, carrying the goods on their back or head. But, nowadays goods are carried by trains, trucks and lorries to other places. People also use boats, steamers and rafts to carry goods to another place.

Boats sail on the rivers, canals and lakes. Ships also carry goods. Cargo ships travel on ocean waters.

People travel from one place to another by car, bus, train and aeroplane. Aeroplanes are the fastest means of transportation. People also travel by ferry boats. Cars and buses are used mainly for short trips. In some cities, there are high-speed trains, which carry passengers to other places.

Underline the Prepositions:

Transportation means the moving of people and goods from one place to another. In earlier days, people walked long distances, carrying the goods on their back or head. But, nowadays goods are carried by trains, trucks and lorries to other places. Boats sail on the rivers, canals and lakes. People travel from one place to another by car, bus, train and aeroplane.

Make sentences of your own:

1) Goods : ____________________

2) Train : ____________________

3) Truck : ____________________

4) Ship : ____________________

5) Boat : ____________________

Strike out (✗) the incorrect option:

1) In earlier days, people travelled......

(a) by rockets (b) on foot

2) They carried their goods on......

(a) their back (b) aeroplanes

3) Cars and buses are used mainly for......

(a) international tours (b) short trips

4) Boats, rafts and steamers sail......

(a) on the rivers (b) in the sky

5) ......are the fastest means of transportation.

(a) bullock carts (b) Aeroplanes

6) Cargo ships travel on......

(a) ocean waters (b) roads

ANSWERS

Page 6

Fill in the blanks:

1) sphere 2) believed 3) travelled, point, started
4) land, water 5) farthest

Page 7

Strike out (✗) the incorrect option:

1) (b) 2) (a) 3) (b) 4) (b) 5) (a) 6) (b)

Page 9

Circle the correct spelling:

1) (a) 2) (b) 3) (c) 4) (a) 5) (c) 6) (a)

Page 10

Answer in one line:

1) The whales belong to a group of animals called marine mammals.

2) People killed whales for their meat and oil.

3) They have a smooth and rubbery skin.

4) Blubber is a layer of fat found beneath the skin.

5) The fat called blubber keeps them warm in cold water.

6) A group of whales is called pod.

Page13

Write True (T) or False (F):

1) (F) 2) (T) 3) (T) 4) (T) 5) (T) 6) (T) 7) (T) 8) (T)

Page 15

Complete the sentences:

1) the dog biscuits and
2) everywhere, wagging his
3) sit on his master's
4) a donkey, who was envious of the dog.
5) decided to play with the
6) master's room, braying loudly.

Page 17

Fill in the blanks:

1) town, cities 2) guard, start
3) control 4) transport
5) Passenger Train 6) workplace

Page 19

Match the following:

1) (c) 2) (d) 3) (a) 4) (e) 5) (h) 6) (g) 7) (f) 8) (b)

Page 22

Fill in the blanks:

1) special 2) drizzling 3) already
4) shivering, umbrella 5) deserted, preferred 6) worried, reached
7) relieved 8) tea 9) blankets
10) happy

Page 24

Strike out(✗) the correct answer:

1) (b) 2) (a) 3) (b) 4) (b) 5) (a)

Page 26

Match the following:

1) (h) 2) (g) 3) (b) 4) (f) 5) (c) 6) (d) 7) (e) 8) (a)

Page 29

Tick (✓) the correct answer:

1) (a) 2) (a) 3) (a) 4) (a) 5) (b)

Page 31

Fill in the blanks:

1) animal, bottom 2) boneless 3) tentacles
4) arms, capture 5) large, head 6) backwards, fluid

Page 33

Write 'RIGHT' or 'WRONG' in the boxes:

1) WRONG 2) RIGHT 3) WRONG
4) WRONG 5) RIGHT 6) RIGHT
7) RIGHT 8) RIGHT

Page 35

Complete the paragraphs:

merchant, Everyday, sacks, donkey, town, cross, stream, water, found, salt, melted, idea, way, again, deliberately

Page37

Make appropriate pairs:

1) (c) 2) (a) 3) (d) 4) (b)

Circle the correct spelling:

1) (c) 2) (a) 3) (a) 4) (c)

Page46

Strike out(✗) the incorrect option:

1) (b) 2) (a) 3) (a) 4) (b) 5) (a) 6) (a)

Page 47

Underline the Articles and Verbs:

A river is a large body of water that flows over the land. A river begins its journey from high mountains or hills. As it flows, it gets more water from streams, lakes, springs, other rivers and rainfall. The end of the river where the water flows into an ocean or lake is called its mouth. Some rivers are very small; they dry up during hot season.

Make at least two meaningful words using the jumbled letters:

1) mount, saint 2) fall, rain 3) spring, sprang
4)water, taller 5) gate, green

Page 49

Fill in the blanks:

1) outdoor 2) racket, ball 3) hollow, heavy
4) two 5)"Doubles" 6) divided, net
7) tournaments 8) excitement

Page 51

Write 'RIGHT' or 'WRONG 'in the boxes:

1) RIGHT 2) WRONG 3) RIGHT
4) WRONG 5) RIGHT 6) RIGHT

Page53

Answer in one line:

1) They had heard lot about the city.
2) Because it was a very hot day.
3) 'Do you see the city?'
4) He saw their village.
5) Because the city looked just like their village.
6) 'It was just like our village.'

Page55

Complete the lines:

1) of the snow
2) how the winds may blow
3) a bird can be
4) are cold and gray
5) his happiest lay
6) the clouds he seems to see
7) too deep for word
8) and all agree

Page 57

Fill in the blanks:

1) neighbour 2) parked, blocking 3) neighbouring
4) babies, people, because 5) leftovers, roadside 6) garbage

Page 59

Match the following:

1) (e) 2) (h) 3) (f) 4) (j) 5) (i) 6) (d) 7) (a) 8) (c) 9) (g) 10) (b)

Page 63

Fill in the blanks:

1) play ground 2) raining, play 3) football, today
4) survive 5) gently 6) cricket, spared, heavy

Page65

Match the following:

1) (h) 2) (e) 3) (d) 4) (c) 5) (b) 6) (g) 7) (f) 8) (a)

Page 67

Answer in one line:

1) A reptile has a dry and scally skin.
2) Some lizards escape from their enemy by changing colour.
3) They move about at night.

Fill in the blanks:

1) lungs
2) water
3) hudred years
4) deserts
5) lizards
6 animals

Page 69

Rearrange the jumbled words and write the lines in the correct order:

1)
I've learned all the tricks
of this wonderful man,
Who has such a regard for the crow,
the crow;

2)
That he lays out his grounds
in a regular plan,
And covers his corn in a row, a row...
Caw, caw, caw!"

Page 71

Answer in one line:

1) He had not eaten any food for many days.
2) He saw an urn full of corn.
3) He became so fat

Complete the paragraph:

food, became, urn, corn, hole, crept, hungry, juicy, stop, finished

Page 73

Write 'RIGHT' or 'WRONG ' in the boxes:

1) RIGHT
2) WRONG
3) RIGHT
4) RIGHT
5) RIGHT
6) RIGHT
7) WRONG
8) WRONG

Page 75

Make at least two meaningful words using the jumbled letters:

1) birth, day
2) send, den
3) seat, sit
4) rate, road

Page 76

Fill in the blanks:

1) Jennie
2) Friday, missing
3) searched
4) father, buy
5) favourite
6) gifts
7) wrapped
8) blue

Page 79

Underline the prepositions:

of, from, to, in, on, or, are, by

Page 80

Strike out (✗) the incorrect option:

1) (a) 2) (b) 3) (a) 4) (b) 5) (a) 6) (b)